Fifty
Sheds
of Grey

Fifty
Sheds
of Grey

C. T. Grey

St. Martin's Griffin
New York

FIFTY SHEDS OF GREY. Copyright © 2012 by 50ShedsofGrey. All rights reserved. Printed in the United States of America. For information, address St. Martin's Press, 175 Fifth Avenue, New York, N.Y. 10010.

www.stmartins.com

The picture acknowledgments on page 144 constitute an extension of this copyright page.

Design by seagulls.net

ISBN 978-1-250-03366-6 (trade paperback)
ISBN 978-1-250-03371-0 (e-book)

First published in Great Britain by Boxtree, an imprint of Pan Macmillan, a division of Macmillan Publishers Limited

10 9 8 7 6 5 4 3

For Dad. And his shed.

'Mr Grey?'

'I keep telling you, Olivia, call me Colin. Mr Grey sounds so formal. Now, what is it?'

'There's someone down here in the lobby, Mr Grey. She says she needs to see you. She says it's urgent.'

I bite my lip, pensively. She? It must be a woman.

'What's her name? Does she have an appointment?'

'No, Mr Grey, and she won't tell me her name, but she's very insistent. She says she knows you.'

I gaze out of the twentieth-floor window at the vast, sprawling metropolis from behind my vast, sprawling desk and frown. Who could it be?

'Very well,' I reply eventually, 'Send her up.'

'Yes, Mr Grey.'

I lay the receiver back on its cradle. As I await my mysterious visitor, my steel grey eyes roll around my vast, sprawling office, entirely white from floor to ceiling apart from a mosaic of small monochrome photographs hanging on the opposite wall – my Fifty Sheds of Grey. One of the pictures catches my attention and my manly lips curve upwards into a wistful smile . . .

I can still feel my knuckles rapping lightly on the heavy oak door of Mellors Manor. There was no reply. I noticed a thick red rope hanging limply from the lintel. I gave it a nervous tug. The door flung open instantly and my eyes were met for the very first time by the shapely, mature figure of Lady Christina Mellors. She was a good fifteen years older than me but even at my tender age I felt something stir. I coughed and, in a timid voice, enquired as to whether there might be any work she needed doing in the grounds of the manor. Her eyes widened and she informed me that her gardener had left for the summer – on gardening leave, apparently – and that with Lord Mellors also away, hunting rare tribes in the Amazon, her garden was in desperate need of a jolly good seeing to. Before I had time to reply, she grabbed my arm and led me to the garden shed. A shed that would change my life for ever . . .

My heart raced to see her lush, overgrown lawn – such a rare and wondrous sight. Nowadays the tendency is for just a small strip or no lawn at all.

I emptied the small water butt for the fifteenth time that day and collapsed, exhausted, into my shed. I like big butts and I cannot lie.

Lady Christina eyed me lasciviously as I removed the last flagstone. That was it – the woman was thoroughly depaved.

It was damp, uncomfortable and didn't last very long but it's true what they say – you never forget your first shed.

Lady Christina bit her lip as she eyed my dripping brush. Somehow I knew it wouldn't be long before I'd be touching up her gazebo.

As she manually adjusted my sprinkler, my inner gardener did a Morris dance of delight.

My eyes watered as I howled with pain. I had learned my first lesson. Never again would I leave a gnome on the garden bench.

Things continued in this playfully innocent fashion until one particularly hot afternoon Lady Christina could wait no longer. Without a word, she grasped me firmly by the hand and led me up the garden path. That fateful day, I went into the shed a boy . . . and came out a man.

I lay back exhausted, gazing happily
out of the shed window. Despite my
concerns about my inexperience,
my rhubarb had come up a treat.

From that first encounter I was hooked – I just couldn't get enough of sheds and mowers. Or S&M for short.

I sigh deeply and take a sip of water. That unforgettable encounter in Lady Christina's garden changed me for ever. It left me with a lifelong love of sheds – and fear of women. That very day I resolved to leave home, find a job and satisfy my cravings as soon as possible.

I lean forward in my large leather chair, scanning the other photographs until finally my eyes rest on the one I'm looking for – the first shed I ever owned. Not much to look at on the outside but filled with many happy memories. Well, memories . . .

'This is a contract between you and me,' she said coolly. I signed shakily. This was it. In twelve easy monthly payments the shed would be mine.

I stared longingly through the shed window and adjusted my trousers. The sight of her dewy, slightly unkempt lawn had awoken my inner gardener.

Over the next few years, I brought an array of weird and wonderful young women to my shed with varying degrees of failure . . .

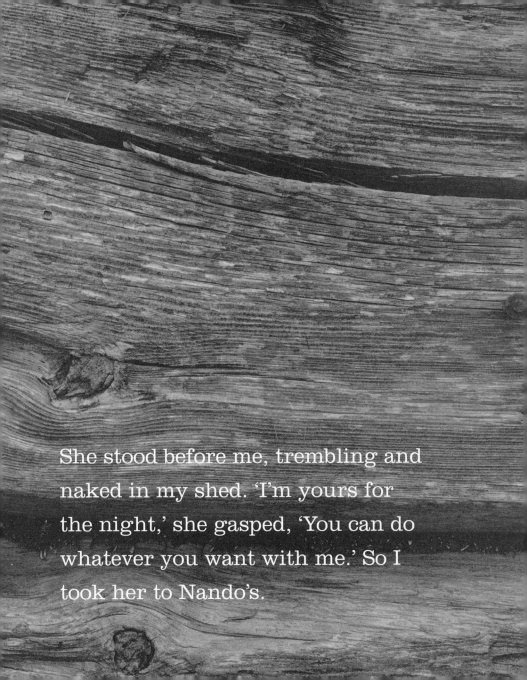

She stood before me, trembling and naked in my shed. 'I'm yours for the night,' she gasped, 'You can do whatever you want with me.' So I took her to Nando's.

She told me she was kinky . . .
so I left the shed light on.

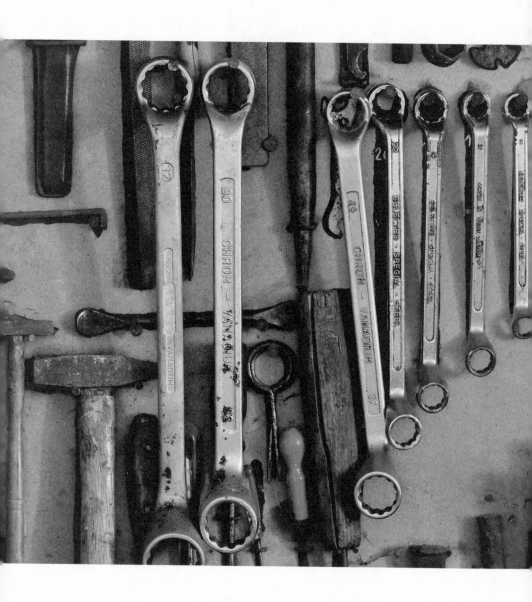

'I do have one fetish,'
I admitted, 'MILFs . . .
Mowers I'd Like to Fix.'

She gazed wide-eyed at the cans stacked precariously against the crimson shed wall. 'Welcome,' I announced proudly, 'to the Red Room of Paint.'

'Meet me in the shed in half an hour wearing only your wellingtons.'
I sighed and put the phone down.
I hated these late-night booty calls.

'Put on this rubber suit and mask,' I instructed, calmly.

'Mmmm . . . kinky,' she purred.

'Yes,' I said, 'Plus you can't be too careful with all that asbestos in the shed roof.'

'Not in this shed,' she said,
'I'm an exhibitionist – I need to
do it somewhere we can be seen.'

I stared at her, horrified. 'Not . . .
the conservatory?'

'No,' she sighed, gazing sadly at the large stuffed crust Hawaiian with extra cheese, 'I said I'm really turned on by orders from dominants.'

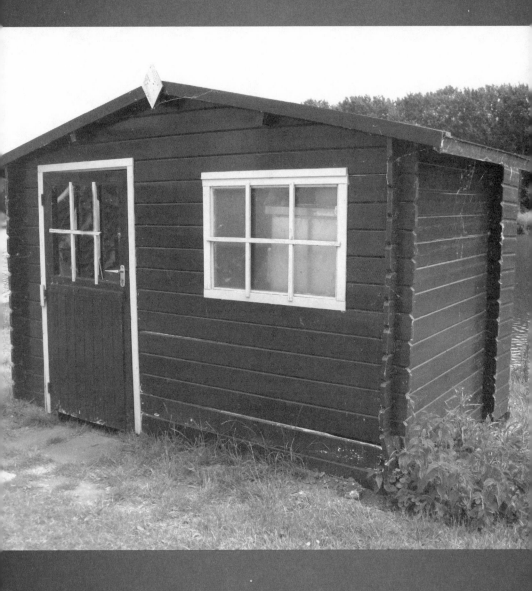

'I think it's time for us to take things to the next level,' she said, eagerly.

'What?' I replied, '. . . the shed roof?'

My eyes dance around the monochrome montage of photographs until finally coming to rest on another, altogether different shed. Increasingly desperate, following a string of distinctly unromantic liaisons, I had come to the obvious conclusion – it must be the shed. It was the Seventies, the time of glam-rock and flares. My poor old brown shed just wasn't cutting it. I had to take action. I took an evening class in shed design and maintenance and before the year was out I had designed and built my very own shed! A friend of mine, a professional decorator, offered to paint it for me. He joked that he should paint it grey to match my name but I was looking for something altogether more eye-catching. When it was finished I stood back to admire its multi-coloured splendour. There was no doubt about it – it was fifty shades of groovy!

Camilla was just one of several young ladies to sample the 'delights' of my Love Shack. I got chatting to her in the local pub and when I mentioned my unusual erection, she said she'd love to take a look and so, after rather a lot of beers and Babychams (I forget what she had), we stumbled eagerly back to my house . . .

A Lighter Shed of Grey

We slipped on the veranda,
Turned cartwheels 'cross the lawn,
I was feeling kind of beer sick,
But I still crawled out for more.
The shed was spinning faster,
And my date began to sway.
When I offered her another drink,
She fainted clean away.

And so it was later,
That Camilla viewed the scene.
And her face at first just yellow,
Turned a lighter shade of green.

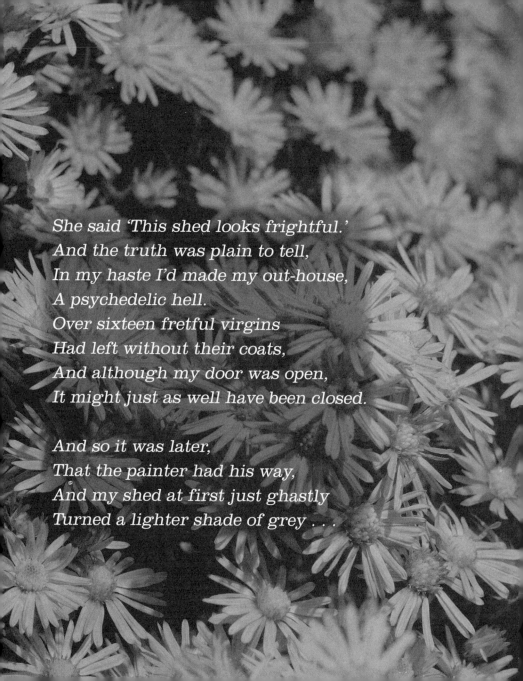

She said 'This shed looks frightful.'
And the truth was plain to tell,
In my haste I'd made my out-house,
A psychedelic hell.
Over sixteen fretful virgins
Had left without their coats,
And although my door was open,
It might just as well have been closed.

And so it was later,
That the painter had his way,
And my shed at first just ghastly
Turned a lighter shade of grey . . .

Sadly, the change of colour didn't prove any more successful. In despair, I turned to poetry but that didn't work either . . .

'Shall I compare thee to a summer-
    house?
Thou art more homely and more
    intimate.
Rough women do shake my darling
    shed of grey,
But summarily spurn a second date.'

However, after many years spent alone with nothing but my poetry and the swimsuit edition of Sheds Illustrated to keep me company, my luck finally changed. Brenda was everything those girls weren't – easily pleased. Our eyes had met across a crowded garden centre. The very next day I took her home to meet my shed

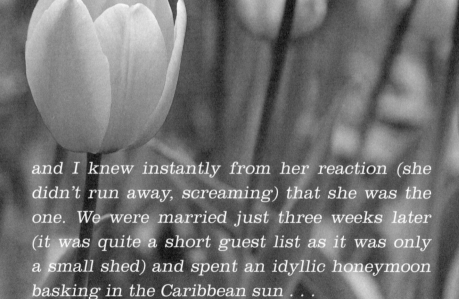

and I knew instantly from her reaction (she didn't run away, screaming) that she was the one. We were married just three weeks later (it was quite a short guest list as it was only a small shed) and spent an idyllic honeymoon basking in the Caribbean sun . . .

We stood alone on the idyllic white beach. She shed her clothes. I shed my inhibitions. At that moment I knew it would always be about sheds.

. . . A gentle tapping jolts me from my sun-kissed reverie. I glance at my office door and straighten my back, ready to greet my mystery visitor.

'Come in,' I call, in a deep, gravelly voice. The door doesn't move.

'Come in,' I repeat, a little deeper and even more gravelly. Still the door doesn't move. I'm bracing myself for my very deepest and most gravelly voice ever when I notice a pigeon sitting on the window ledge. He cocks his head quizzically at me then taps the glass with his tiny beak. I smile at him and give him a wink, then frown at my 96-diamond platinum Rolex. Where has this woman got to? It must be a quarter of an hour since the call.

'Hello . . . Olivia? Did you send that woman up? She hasn't arrived yet.'

The voice on the line answers in the affirmative.

'Strange . . . ' I reply, 'Oh well, could you reschedule my three o'clock? Thank you. Oh, and can you call the exterminators? The pigeons are back.'

I stroke my chin. Maybe she's changed her mind. I should get back to work – I don't want to waste the whole afternoon waiting for somebody not to come. I look at my computer screen and place my long, sturdy fingers on the keyboard but somehow my eyes are drawn back to the photographs on the wall and one in particular. Our first shed together . . .

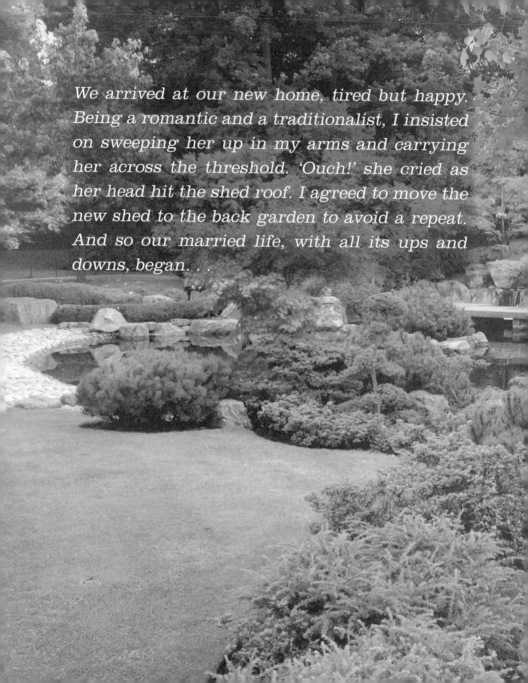

We arrived at our new home, tired but happy. Being a romantic and a traditionalist, I insisted on sweeping her up in my arms and carrying her across the threshold. 'Ouch!' she cried as her head hit the shed roof. I agreed to move the new shed to the back garden to avoid a repeat. And so our married life, with all its ups and downs, began. . .

We tried various positions – round the back, on the side, up against a wall . . . but in the end we came to the conclusion that the bottom of the garden was the only place for a really good shed.

She knelt before me on the shed
floor and tugged gently at first,
then harder until finally it came.
I moaned with pleasure. Now for
the other boot . . .

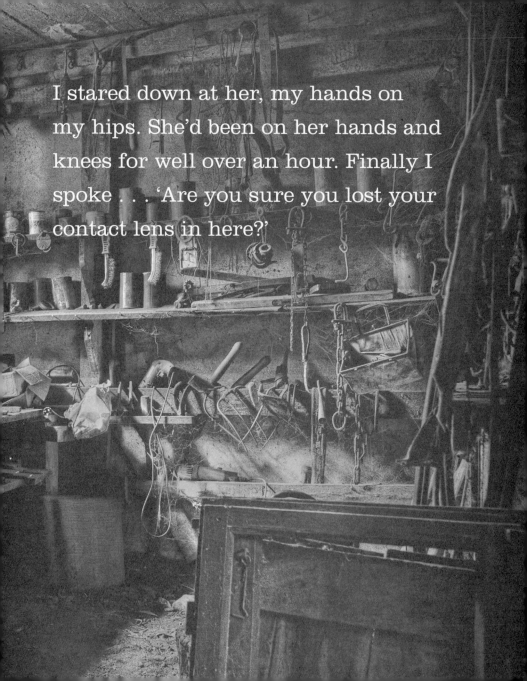

I stared down at her, my hands on my hips. She'd been on her hands and knees for well over an hour. Finally I spoke . . . 'Are you sure you lost your contact lens in here?'

'Harder,' she cried, gripping the workbench tightly, 'Harder!'

'Alright,' I said. 'What's the gross national product of Nicaragua?'

My body writhed and quivered from the pain. I had learned my next lesson. Never again would I leave an upturned plug on the shed floor.

'Are you sure you want this?'
I asked. 'When I'm done you won't
be able to sit down for weeks.'

She nodded.

'Okay,' I said, putting the three-piece
suite on eBay.

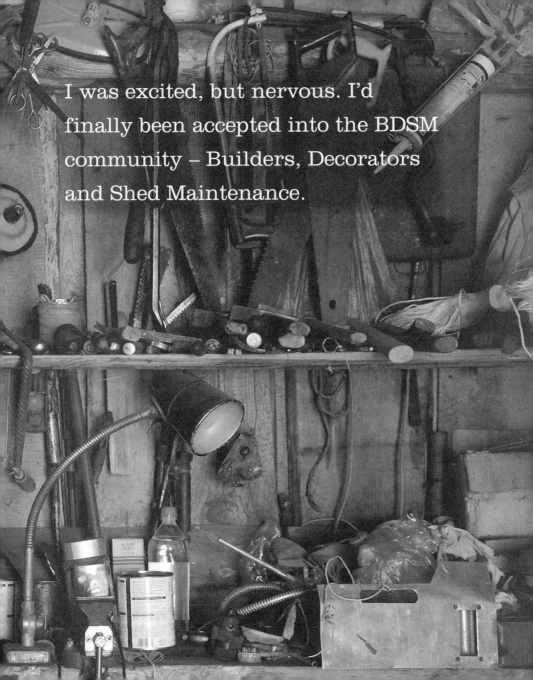

I was excited, but nervous. I'd finally been accepted into the BDSM community – Builders, Decorators and Shed Maintenance.

As I stared out at the army of strange creatures standing to attention on the lawn, I realized I'd mixed up the slug pellets and the Viagra.

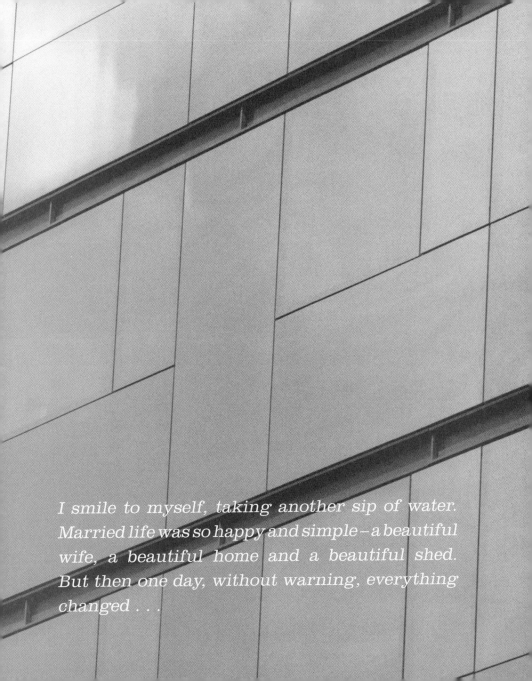

I smile to myself, taking another sip of water.
Married life was so happy and simple – a beautiful
wife, a beautiful home and a beautiful shed.
But then one day, without warning, everything
changed . . .

The soft, rhythmic motion rocked me gently as I headed home that day, blissfully unaware of what lay in wait. I looked blearily around the train carriage at my fellow commuters, the men nose-deep in their broadsheets, the women staring wide-eyed and rosy-cheeked at their paperbacks. I wondered what type of literature could be evoking such a flushed response. On closer inspection I was surprised to see that all of their books bore the same cover – a silver knotted tie on a dark background. My brow furrowed. Were today's women really so fascinated by male formal attire? I was clearly out of touch – perhaps I should ask my own dear Brenda. However, when I arrived home I was surprised to find a letter waiting for me on the dining table: 'Your dinner's in the supermarket.' I called her name but there was no reply. I searched every room until finally I found her, lying in the bath, surrounded by scented candles, reading THAT book. From that moment things would never be the same again . . .

'Punish me,' she cried desperately, 'Make me suffer like only a real man can!'

'Very well,' I replied, leaving the toilet seat up.

She told me it turned her on to have her movements restricted when she made love. I looked around – I was going to have to get a smaller shed.

'Are you sure you can take
the pain?' she demanded,
brandishing her stilettos.

'I think so,' I gulped.

'Here we go, then,' she said,
and showed me the receipt.

'Pleasure and pain can be experienced simultaneously,' she said, gently massaging my back as we listened to her Coldplay CD.

'Now,' she said, fiercely, 'I'm going to take you by the collar and lead you naked round the garden.'

I was shocked – the poor vicar had only popped round for a cup of tea.

My whole body shuddered as she entered my Man Cave. I really must get a padlock for the shed door.

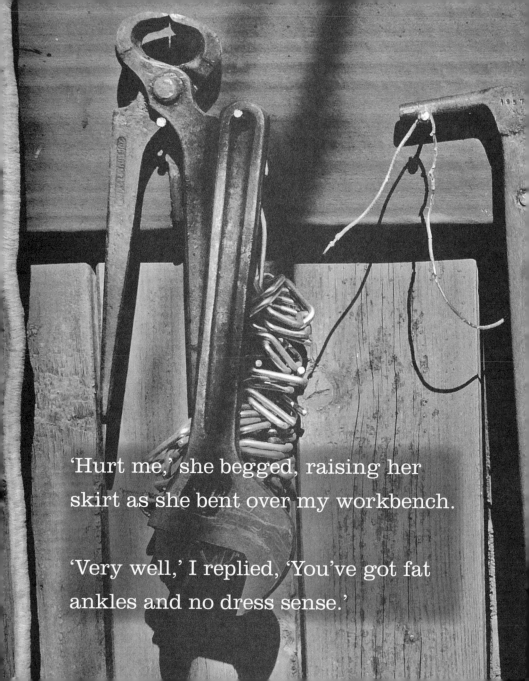

'Hurt me,' she begged, raising her skirt as she bent over my workbench.

'Very well,' I replied, 'You've got fat ankles and no dress sense.'

Ever since she read THAT book, I've had to buy all kinds of ropes, chains and shackles. She still manages to get into the shed though.

'Happy birthday,' she said, placing a riding crop in my hand and lowering her skirt, 'Today's your lucky day'. I couldn't believe it – I was getting a pony!

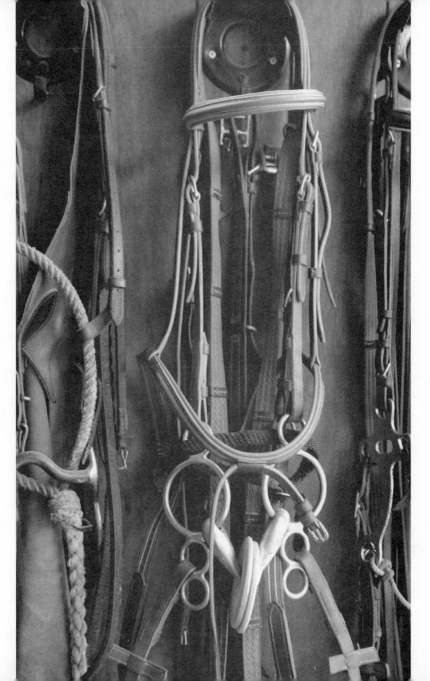

I froze when I saw the room full of masks, saddles and oddly-shaped battery-powered devices. That was it – no more drunk-ebaying for me.

She gazed up at me wide-eyed
from the shed floor and bit her lip
seductively. Unfortunately it was her
top lip so she looked like a piranha.

By the time I'd finished, her bottom
was bright pink – I'd mixed up
the baby oil and Thousand Island
dressing again.

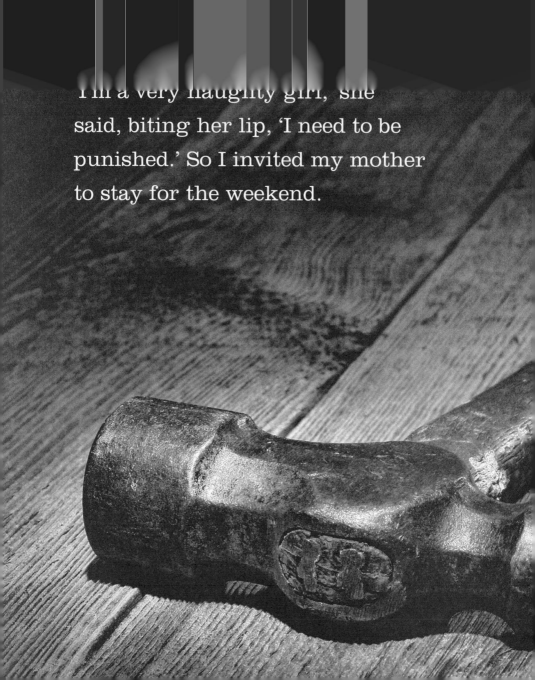

I'm a very naughty girl,' she said, biting her lip, 'I need to be punished.' So I invited my mother to stay for the weekend.

'I am your master,' I commanded, 'You will obey my rules.' She rolled her eyes and walked out of the shed. That was definitely it – I needed to get a new cat.

As we stood there naked in Ikea, we came to an important decision. Next time only one of us would wear a blindfold.

'Make me feel pain like I've never felt before,' she pleaded, blindfolded and naked.

'Alright,' I said, placing the Lego bricks on the shed floor . . .

'Yes, mistress,' I replied. I didn't dare argue as I bent over the workbench – I could see she had a strop on. At least, I think that's what they're called.

I told her exactly what she should do in my sternest and most dominant voice and awaited her response. Finally it came. 'Please hold the line. Your call is very important to us . . . '

As we were discharged from the casualty department for the third time that month, we began to wonder whether we should change the safe word from Llanfairpwllgwyngyllgogerychwyrndrobwllllantysiliogogogoch.

We each dropped our keys into the bowl. Before long we'd be entering a world of forbidden delights. God, I loved those shed-swapping parties.

So this was it – it was really going to happen. Every man's ultimate fantasy . . . Three In A Shed.

I managed to stay calm as my wife expertly bound my wrists and ankles. Although I have to admit I did get a little nervous when she bundled me into the boot of the car . . .

'You're obsessed!' she cried, slamming the door as she stormed out, 'You love this shed more than me!' I frowned. Obsessed? Me? Ridiculous! Shed be back. I mean, she'd be back . . .

But she wasn't. Brenda never returned and once more I was alone. I retreated into my shed. I sought solace in my garden and the World Wide Web. I tried dating and social networking sites, soon becoming quite proficient at the lingo. It didn't take me long to figure out the acronyms (PMSL – Painting My Shed Lovingly, LMAO – Lawn Mowers Are Okay) but for some reason, none of these sites yielded a companion. I gave up and found myself drawn to the darker corners of the internet and immersed myself in a twilight world of garden-based erotica, tawdry one-night sheds and online movies such as Last Tango in Homebase, The Red Shed Diaries and 9½ Weeds . . . I stared around the shed Brenda and I had modified, and sighed. I stroked the leather studded workbench sadly. And then suddenly it came to me . . .

I stare at the photograph in the very centre of the group. Our shed. The one I eventually agreed to convert into our 'playroom'. The one that sat empty for years until the day I inexplicably found myself opening its door again, looked around at the chains hanging sadly from the walls, stroked the leather studded workbench and . . . had an idea. Not just an idea. The idea. The idea that was to make my name. The idea that gave me this vast, sprawling desk in this vast, sprawling office and three quarters of this vast, sprawling metropolis. I walk slowly over to the door and open it to look at the brass plate affixed to the other side.

'Colin T. Grey, CEO, Slea-Z-Sheds International'.

I brush the gleaming brass with the cuff of my Armani suit and my face breaks into a proud and slightly sad smile.

'Hello.'

I swivel round then immediately freeze, my heart pounding. I can't believe what I'm seeing. After all this time. After all those sheds. Finally my open mouth begins to form words.

'What . . are you . . doing here?'

'Ssssshh . .' she whispers, placing her finger over my lips.

'But . . . It's been so long,'

'I know,' she says softly, 'the elevator was broken.'

'No, I mean . . .'

'I wanted to wait . . . until the time was right.' She reaches into her purse and draws out a blindfold. 'Come with me,' she says raising it to my eyes.

I roll my eyes and bite my lip. Just when I thought I had finally reached a lighter shade of Grey, I can see that, once again, things are about to get darker . . .

Picture Acknowledgements

Page 10 © Ron Evans/Getty images, 23 © Charles Gullung/Getty Images, 26 © Steven Miric/Getty Images, 41 © PhotoAlto/Neville Mountford-Hoare/ Getty Images, 81 © Lynn Keddie/Getty Images.

The following images are used under license from Shutterstock.com, 2012:

Pages 6 and 7 © Vladitto, 8 and 9 © Dragan Jovanovic, 13 © Chrislofoto, 14 © Jeff Gynane, 17 © Stock Creative, 18 © Whytock, 20 and 21 © mashe, 24 and 25 © Eky Studio, 29 © Theresasc75, 30 and 31 © Digitaldepth, 33 © Jeff Dalton, 34 © PHB.cz (Richard Semik), 36 and 37 © SCOTTCHAN, 38 and 39 © BlackHead, 42 © meanmachine77, 45 © Vincent St. Thomas, 46 © Zbynek Jirousek, 48 and 49 © gary718, 50 © Andrew Park, 53 © B474, 54 and 55 © Jan Krcmar, 56 and 57 © Eky Studio, 58 and 59 © Olena Mykhaylova, 60 and 61 © jennyt, 62 © perlphoto, 64 and 65 © Denis Tabler, 67 © Jo Crebbin, 68 and 69 © a454, 70 and 71 © r.nagy, 72 © cycreation, 75 © Larisa Lofitskaya, 76 and 77 © glo, 78 © Els Jooren, 82 © BONNIE WATTON, 84 and 85 © Polryaz, 87 © Andrew Haddon, 88 and 89 © Péter Gudella, 90 and 91 © Chrislofoto, 92 © shippee, 95 © South 12th Photography, 97 © David Hughes, 98 © Rod Ferris, 101 © Antonina Potapenko, 102 © Tupungato, 104 and 105 © Oleinikova Olga, 106 © Marafona, 109 © holbox, 110 © Carlos Caetano, 113 © Neale Cousland, 114 © V. J. Matthew, 116 and 117 © Olivier Le Queinec, 118 © Chrislofoto, 121 © Richard Evans, 122 and 123 © Becky Stares, 125 © Simon Bratt, 126 © Jason Vandehey, 128 and 129 © Imageman, 130 © dinadesign, 133 © zhuhe2343603, 134 © Vasil Vasilev, 137 © c.byatt-norman, 138 and 139 © c.byatt-norman, 140 © Dawid Konopka.